D0501551

© 2000 by Barbour Publishing, Inc.

ISBN 1-57748-710-9

Cover art © Photodisc, Inc.

All rights reserved. No part of this publication may be reproduced or transmitted in any form or by any means without written permission of the publisher.

Scripture quotations are taken from the *Holy Bible,* New Living Translation, copyright © 1996. Used by permission of Tyndale House Publishers, Inc., Wheaton, Illinois 60189, U.S.A. All rights reserved.

Published by Humble Creek, P. O. Box 719, Uhrichsville, Ohio 44683

ecpa Member of the
Evangelical Christian
Publishers Association

Printed in China.

Go for the Goal

written and compiled by
Daniel Partner

HUMBLECREEK
INSPIRATION FOR LIFE

Ah, but a man's reach
should exceed his grasp,
Or what's a heaven for?

Robert Browning

GO FOR THE GOAL IN BLESSING

And God will generously provide all you need.
Then you will always have everything you need
and plenty left over to share with others. . . .
For God is the one who gives seed to
the farmer and then bread to eat.
In the same way, he will give you many
opportunities to do good,
and he will produce a
great harvest of generosity in you.

Paul, from 2 Corinthians 9:8, 10

Look to your health;
and if you have it, praise God,
and value it next to a good conscience;
for health is the second blessing
that we mortals are capable of;
a blessing that money cannot buy.

Izaak Walton

Dave Dravecky's Comeback

More than a decade has passed since Dave Dravecky last pitched in a major league baseball game. But his fame may be even greater now than when he was an All-Star athlete at the top of his profession.

Born on Valentine's Day, 1956, near Youngstown, Ohio, Dave Dravecky achieved the dream of millions of boys around the world by becoming a big-league ballplayer. He arrived in the majors in 1982 with the San Diego Padres, going 5–3 with a fine 2.57 ERA in his rookie season.

In his next season, Dravecky made the All-Star team, and the following year, was pitching in the World Series. Three years later, pitching better than ever, he was traded to San Francisco, where his world would soon change dramatically.

A cancerous tumor in his pitching arm led to the removal of half of his deltoid muscle, and doctors doubted he would ever play baseball again. But through much hard work, Dravecky did return to the field, pitching a triumphant 4–3 win over Cincinnati in August, 1989. Baseball fans will never forget his next game, however, when Dravecky's arm snapped while throwing a pitch against Montreal. The cancer was back, and eventually cost Dravecky his entire left arm and shoulder.

To many, it would seem a crushing blow—to have returned to the game he loved, only to be forced away permanently by one of the most dreaded diseases of all. But that viewpoint fails to account for Dave Dravecky's strong faith in God.

About six years before, Dravecky had accepted Jesus Christ through the witness of a minor-league teammate. The peace and comfort that only God can provide helped Dave and his wife, Jan, through the rigors of his medical treatment and amputation, and the subsequent depression that each faced.

Through the wise words of another Christian ballplayer, Dravecky came to realize that his biggest miracle wasn't returning to the game after cancer—it was the salvation that he had through Christ. God had given Dravecky fame through baseball, and now Dave would use his position to lead others to Jesus. "When I think about that, I'm overwhelmed," Dravecky says in "Hope in the Midst of Adversity" (http://www.lifestory.org/drav2.html). "You know what? This cancer's really been a blessing. It's unbelievable."

The man who posted a career ERA of 3.13 now pitches the love of God—through his ministry of motivational speaking. He has either written or contributed to several books, including *Comeback* and *When You Can't Come Back,* and maintains a website entitled "Dave Dravecky's Outreach of Hope—A Ministry of Encouragement" (http://www.dravecky.org).

Dave Dravecky has enjoyed the pinnacles of earthly success, and suffered the greatest valleys as well. But he knows God sends them all for a reason. Psalm 34:18 headlines his home page: "The Lord is near to the brokenhearted, and saves those who are crushed in spirit."

Reflect upon your present blessings
of which every man has many;
not on your past misfortunes
of which all men have some.

Charles Dickens

Clear Goals—
Simple Decisions

Jesus knew where He had come from, why He was here, and what He was supposed to accomplish. He came down from heaven, not to do His own will, but the will of the Father. That determination controlled every decision He made.

As a result He was not distracted with trivia. He was never in a hurry, for He knew His Father would not give a task without the time to do it. Christ was not driven by crises, feeling He must heal everyone in Israel. He could say, "It is finished," even when many people were still bound by demons and twisted by disease. What mattered ultimately was not the number of people healed or fed, but whether the Father's will was being done. His clearly defined goals simplified His decisions.

Erwin W. Lutzer

Go for the Goal in Work

Work brings profit,
but mere talk leads to poverty!

Solomon, from Proverbs 14:23

It is not only prayer that
gives God glory but work.
Smiting on an anvil, sawing a beam,
whitewashing a wall, driving horses,
sweeping, scouring,
everything gives God glory if
being in His grace you do it as your duty.
To go to Communion worthily
gives God great glory,
but to take food in thankfulness
and temperance gives Him glory too.
To lift up the hands in prayer gives God glory,
but a man with a dung fork in his hand,
a woman with a slop pail, gives Him glory too.
He is so great that all things
give Him glory if you mean they should.

Gerard Manley Hopkins

The best things are nearest:
breath in your nostrils,
light in your eyes, flowers at your feet,
duties at your hand,
the path of God just before you.
Then do not grasp at the stars,
but do life's plain, common work as it comes.

Robert Louis Stevenson

Every task, however simple
sets the soul that does it free;
Every deed of human kindness
done in love is done to Thee.
Jesus, Thou divine companion,
help us all to work our best;
Bless us in our daily labor,
lead us to our Sabbath rest.

Henry Van Dyke

When God put Adam and Eve in the garden,
He did not put them there to sit and
look at each other and to hold hands.
He said they were to take care of the garden.
You remember that—
they were given something to do.
Some people believe that work is
a result of the curse,
but that's not true.
The idea is abroad that the man
who works is a boob,
and that work is only for fools—
but God made us to work.

A. W. Tozer, from *Who Put Jesus on the Cross?*

Go for the Goal in Growth

The godly will flourish like palm trees
and grow strong like the cedars of Lebanon.
For they are transplanted into
the Lord's own house.
They flourish in the courts of our God.
Even in old age they will still produce fruit;
they will remain vital and green.
They will declare,
"The Lord is just! He is my rock!
There is nothing but goodness in him!"

An anonymous poet of ancient Israel,
from Psalm 92:12–15

I now enjoy Tolstoy and Jane Austen
and Trollope as well as fairy tales
and I call that growth:
if I had to lose the fairy tales
in order to acquire the novelists,
I would not say that I had grown
but only that I had changed.
A tree grows because it adds rings:
a train doesn't grow by leaving
one station behind
and puffing on to the next.

C. S. Lewis,
from *Of Other Worlds: Essays and Stories*

Growing into the Knowledge of God

Bruce Cockburn is a Canadian singer-songwriter, long popular in Canada, and well-known in the U.S. He is a Christian, as are many of his fans.

Although religion had been a part of his childhood, it was very cold and formal. "I went to Sunday school as a kid because it was a social convention," he recalls. "My parents were agnostic and still are, yet they sent us to church because they did not want the neighbors to think we were weird. . . . So I grew up surrounded by the imagery and hearing the stories, but not having it charged with any meaning."

After dropping out of high school and busking (a busker is a street musician) in Europe, he went to the Berklee College of Music in Boston for a year and a half. There he studied music composition (1964–1966). Cockburn says he didn't finish college because he realized he couldn't put in the required effort.

In his early twenties, Cockburn started a personal spiritual search. He flirted with Buddhism and even the occult, and was quite surprised when his search led him to Jesus Christ.

This began when he read C. S. Lewis's allegorical children's tales *The Chronicles of Narnia* and climaxed with an experience of Christ at his own church wedding. "At the moment we were saying our vows," says Cockburn, "there was an overwhelming impression that there was someone standing there that I could not see. . . . It was Jesus. All of a sudden it hit me, 'Oh, so we aren't talking just about books here, we are talking about something very tangible.' "

Cockburn is a fine guitar player and cites many guitarists as influences: Wes Montgomery, Brownie McGhee, Mississippi John Hurt, Mance Lipscomb, Gabor Szabo, and Jimi Hendrix ("not so much for what he was doing as how loud he did it"). One of Bruce's early bands opened for Hendrix in Montreal in 1968. "It was an interesting glimpse of fame, looking at him looking at the people looking at him. The whole 'star phenomenon' was very strange—I certainly didn't want it to happen to me. I don't worry about that anymore," Cockburn laughs.

With over twenty-five albums to his credit, Cockburn's most recent release is "Breakfast in New Orleans, Dinner in Timbuktu" (Rykodisc). On September 5, 1997, Bruce Cockburn went back to college: He delivered the commencement speech at the Berklee College of Music, his old school, and was given an honorary degree of doctor of music.

That no obedience but
a perfect one will satisfy God,
I hold with all my heart and strength;
but that there is none else that He cares for,
is one of the lies of the enemy.
What father is not pleased with the
first tottering attempt of his little one to walk?
What father would be satisfied with anything
but the manly step of the full-grown son?

George Macdonald

Your faith will produce a life of
moral excellence.
A life of moral excellence
leads to knowing God better.
Knowing God leads to self-control.
Self-control leads to patient endurance,
and patient endurance leads to godliness.
Godliness leads to love for other Christians,
and finally you will grow to
have genuine love for everyone.
The more you grow like this,
the more you will become productive
and useful in your knowledge of
our Lord Jesus Christ.

Peter, from 2 Peter 1:5–8

Now, while the antler of the eaves
Liquefies, drop by drop, I brood
On a Christian thing: unless the leaves
Perish, the tree is not renewed.

If all our perishable stuff
Be nourished to its root, we clean
Our trunk of death, and in our tough
And final growth are evergreen.

Stanley Kunitz

Go for the Goal in Education

He was in the Temple,
sitting among the religious teachers,
discussing deep questions with them.

Luke, from Luke 2:46

See some good picture—in nature, if possible,
or on a canvas—hear a page of the best music,
or read a great poem every day.
You will always find a free half hour
for one or the other,
and at the end of the year your mind will
shine with such an accumulation of jewels
as will astonish even yourself.

Henry Wadsworth Longfellow

Whom, then, do I call educated?
First, those who control circumstances
instead of being mastered by them,
those who meet all occasions manfully
and act in accordance with intelligent thinking,
those who are honorable in all dealings,
who treat good-naturedly persons and
things that are disagreeable; and furthermore,
those who hold their pleasures under control
and are not overcome by misfortune;
finally, those who are not spoiled by success.

Socrates

The wisest mind has something yet to learn.

George Santayana

The more we learn the more we realize
how little we know.

R. Buckminster Fuller

Go for the Goal in Service

The only thing they suggested was that we
remember to help the poor,
and I have certainly been eager to do that.

Paul, from Galatians 2:10

Small service is true service while it lasts:
Of humblest friends, bright creature,
scorn not one:
The daisy, by the shadow that it casts,
Protects the lingering dewdrop
from the sun.

William Wordsworth

An Introduction to a Servant

"We are made to live in a delicate network of interdependence with one another," writes Desmond Tutu in the introduction to *An African Prayer Book*. He continues: "We say in our African idiom: 'A person is a person through other persons.' A solitary human being is a contradiction in terms. . . . I have gifts that you do not; and you have gifts that I do not. Voilà! So we need each other to become fully human." Desmond Tutu is many things, but he is certainly not solitary. Instead he has devoted his gifts to serve the spiritual and temporal needs of humanity.

Desmond Mpilo Tutu was born in 1931 in Klerksdorp, Transvaal (southern Africa). His father was a teacher. Tutu was educated at Johannesburg Bantu High School and trained as a teacher at Pretoria Bantu Normal College. In 1954 he graduated from the University of South Africa.

Next he worked three years as a high school teacher. Then Tutu began to study theology and was ordained as an Anglican priest in 1960. From 1962 to 1966 he was devoted to further theological study in England and earned a master of theology from Kings College, Oxford. From 1967 to 1972 he taught theology in South Africa before returning to England for three years as the assistant director of a theological institute in London.

He was named Dean of Johannesburg in 1975 (the first black to hold that position) and Bishop of Lesotho in 1977. The following year, he became the first black general secretary of the South African Council of Churches. In 1984 Bishop Tutu was awarded the Nobel Peace Prize in recognition of "the courage and heroism shown by black South Africans in their use of peaceful methods in the struggle against apartheid."

Apartheid, South Africa's system of racial separatism, has since been dismantled, thanks in part to the outspoken leadership and spiritual ministry of Desmond Tutu.

He is the author of *The Rainbow People of God* and *An African Prayer Book,* and recipient of more than twenty honorary doctorates and numerous other international awards.

By all accounts, Tutu is just as Christopher Ahrends, Acting Dean of the Church of the Province of Southern Africa, has said:

> Archbishop Desmond, for all that he is and has done, stands out in my mind as a modern example of one who has allowed God to use what God gave him at birth. He has lived for others. He, at some point, said yes, and discovered in a flash everywhere around him, the one thing necessary. And God sighed with relief and was able (once again) to be present in the world and make this world more like the world God would have it be.

Wherever a man turns,
he can find someone who needs him.

Albert Schweitzer

The heart is happiest when
it beats for others.

Unknown

The greatest among you
must be a servant.

Jesus Christ, from Matthew 23:11

[Jesus Christ's] idea is that we serve him
by being the servants of other men. . . .
He says that in his kingdom he that is greatest
shall be the servant of all.

Oswald Chambers

Go for the Goal in Character

My dear son,
be strong with the special favor
God gives you in Christ Jesus.

Paul, from 2 Timothy 2:1

Our greatest need today is not more
Christianity but more true Christians.
The world can argue against
Christianity as an institution,
but there is no convincing argument
against a person who,
through the spirit of God,
has been made Christ-like.

Billy Graham

A Faith to Die For

On January 9, 1956, an airplane searched for five young Americans in the wilderness of Ecuador. On a sandbar on the Curaray River, near the headwaters of the Amazon, the pilot spotted a yellow Piper aircraft; objects were strewn about, a body floated in the river. Later, on land, a search party found that the five missionaries had been killed by the primitive people they were trying to reach with the good news of Jesus Christ.

The Aucas had many times before used their nine-foot spears to repel outsiders—from Spanish conquistadors of the sixteenth century to prospectors for oil companies. On this day their spears had made modern Christian martyrs.

Who were these five men who died for the cause of the gospel?

* Jim Elliot—zealous, intense, and intellectually gifted, with interests ranging over public speaking, music, art, literature, and poetry. He was a college wrestling champion.

* Pete Fleming—youngest of the five, with a passion for Scripture, a Christian at age thirteen. Pete earned a

master's degree to sharpen his intellect for
language studies.

* Ed McCully—star football player, oratory
  champion, class president. Law school promised
  him even more success. Instead Ed abandoned
  his life to God's service.

* Nate Saint—the pilot of the team, who used his
  technical skills for an eternal purpose.

* Roger Younderian - World War II paratrooper
  who had overcome polio as a boy. He was a
  pioneer missionary to the famous head-shrinking
  Jivaros Indians.

What was their purpose—the goal which was worth dying for?
Like the Apostle Paul, another missionary from long ago, they
wanted "to preach the Good News where the name of Christ has
never been heard. . .where it says:

Those who have never
been told about him will see,
and those who have never
heard of him will understand."

Romans 15:21

Read the story of a man whose passion was the gospel in *Shadow of the Almighty: The Life and Testament of Jim Elliot* by Elisabeth Elliot.

What lies behind us
and what lies before us
are tiny matters compared to
what lies within us.

Ralph Waldo Emerson

St. Augustine's Goal

Augustine was a theologian of the early church who lived from 354 to 430. He is still a figure of major importance to the church and to the world in general. But he was more than this. He was a seeker of God.

His mother, Monica, was a Christian. His father, Patrick, was a pagan. Together they lived in northern Africa. Beginning his quest at age seventeen, Augustine moved to Carthage, where he says, "A caldron of unholy loves bubbled up all around me." He took a mistress, had a son by her, and joined the heretical Manichaean sect. He later wrote that he "rushed on headlong into such blindness, that amongst my equals I was ashamed to be less shameless."

In Milan the young man was attracted to the preaching of a famous Christian teacher named Ambrose. Augustine became a Christian when reading Romans 13:13–14: "We should be decent and true in everything we do, so that everyone can approve of our behavior. Don't participate in wild parties and getting drunk, or in adultery and immoral living; or in fighting and jealousy. But let the Lord Jesus Christ take control of you, and don't think of ways to indulge your evil desires." He and his son were baptized by Ambrose on Easter, 387.

Augustine returned to North Africa in 388, became priest to the church at Hippo, and bishop in 396. When the Barbarians sacked Rome in 410, pagans blamed the fall of the city on the Christians who had deserted the old Roman gods. Christians were caught in a bind—they had claimed that God would protect the empire of the Christian emperors. Refugees who reached North Africa demanded an explanation from Augustine. He answered by writing *City of God,* the seminal, systematic, biblical view of history and the state. It gave the bewildered, nearly hopeless church new confidence in God.

By the year 430 Roman North Africa had been destroyed by the Barbarians along with much of Latin Christianity and Hippo was held in military siege. At this time Augustine ministered to a congregation swelling with refugees, melted the church's gold vessels to raise funds for their needs, contracted a fatal disease, and died.

This man gave us so much: In addition to *City of God,* Augustine's autobiography, *Confessions,* provides a biblical understanding of a person's life under grace. He was the first to explain the concept of the church. He clarified the church's understanding of Christ. He made God's grace the theme of western theology. Yet his personal goal was quite simple. He expressed it in this prayer:

This only do I ask of your extreme kindness.
That you convert me wholly to yourself
and you allow nothing to prevent me
from wending my way to you.